PROTECTING THE PLANET FROM CLIMATE CHANGE

What's the weather like today? Some days are sunny and some are rainy. The weather over a long period of time is called climate.

The world's climate has always changed. At the moment our planet is getting hotter faster than ever before. It is mostly caused by human activities such as burning coal and oil, and cutting down forests that help keep the Earth cool.

Ice sheets are melting, oceans are getting warmer, deserts are getting larger and there are more hurricanes and tropical storms. People and animals have to find safer places to live. When one animal or plant moves or disappears from its habitat, the lives of other species that depend on it change too.

Climate change is upsetting the balance of nature and threatening the most amazing places on Earth.

But you can help and together we can protect our planet.

With thanks to:

***Dr Mike Murray-Hudson, Associate Professor, University
of Botswana (Okavango Research Institute)***

***Dr Rainer von Brandis, Research Director, National
Geographic Okavango Wilderness Project***

***My friend Robyn Sheldon who lives in the Okavango and
long ago made my first visit to the delta possible.***

First published 2023 by Walker Books Ltd
87 Vauxhall Walk, London SE11 5HJ

2 4 6 8 10 9 7 5 3 1

Text © 2023 Catherine Barr
Illustrations © 2023 Jean Claude

This book has been typeset in Rockwell

Printed in China

British Library Cataloguing in Publication Data:
a catalogue record for this book is available from the British Library

ISBN 978-1-4063-9968-4

www.walker.co.uk

LET'S SAVE
THE OKAVANGO DELTA
WHY WE MUST PROTECT OUR PLANET

CATHERINE BARR   JEAN CLAUDE

WALKER BOOKS
AND SUBSIDIARIES
LONDON · BOSTON · SYDNEY · AUCKLAND

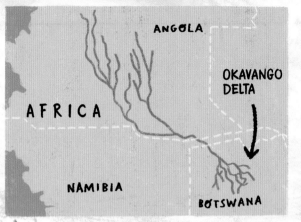

The Okavango Delta in southern Africa is one of the most spectacular wetland habitats on Earth. A delta is usually formed when a river slows down and fans out as it reaches the sea. But the Okavango River empties into the Kalahari Desert, creating a rare inland delta. The water in the Okavango Delta never reaches the sea, but simply trickles away into the sand.

Rain falls on distant high ground in Angola and fills the Okavango River. The river flows across Angola and Namibia, before fanning out into a delta in Botswana. Every year, thousands of birds and animals travel to the watery paradise of the Okavango Delta. But the delta is dangerously dependent on its distant water supply, which is threatened by human activities and climate change.

Let's find out why we must save the Okavango Delta.

Let's save the Okavango Delta

because of its spectacular seasonal swamps.

When the rain water from Angola pulses into the Okavango Delta, the delta's wetlands double in size. Water surges beyond the permanent swamp, over the surrounding grassland and sand. This creates new waterways and sparkling lagoons, and the flooded delta bursts into life. But in time, under the scorching sun, the floodwater dries up and the animals move on, to return again the following year.

Every year at the start of the seasonal flood, around twenty thousand large animals including wildebeest, zebra, buffalo and elephants arrive looking for food and water.

The delta's plants and animals have adapted their life-cycles to the annual cycle of rains and flooding. If the rains and floods change, they could be at risk.

Once all the water dries up, people set fire to the dusty grassland so new shoots grow in the ash. This clears land for farming. The fresh grass feeds farm animals and attracts wildlife for hunting.

As the floodwater dries up and the wetlands shrink, thirsty herds of animals move away towards the smell of rain.

Let's save the Okavango Delta

because it's the greatest wildlife show on Earth.

Some of the world's most endangered species, from black rhinos to pangolins, seek safety in the Okavango Delta. Every year, their home is transformed as the floodwater rises. Huge herds of wildlife travel to the delta in some of the last great animal migrations on Earth. The wetlands become crowded with life.

Packs of rare wild dogs, also called painted dogs because of their patchwork coats, splash through the swamps to bring down their prey.

Mayflies, midges and termites are important sources of food for animals, birds and reptiles.

The delta is a protected **UNESCO** World Heritage Site because of the incredible diversity of its plant and animal life.

Mega herds of up to **500** elephants – the largest elephant herds on Earth – have been tracked by scientists flying over the delta.

Let's save the Okavango Delta

because it's an **ancient homeland**.

Indigenous communities have lived alongside the Okavango River since ancient times. They rely on its fresh water to wash, cook and drink, and on the floods for plentiful fish and wildlife to hunt. Using skills and knowledge passed down through the generations, these diverse communities know how to avoid dangerous animals and find plants for medicine and food. Their way of life depends on the seasonal cycles of this huge wetland.

Most traditional communities build their homes along the drier land at the edges of the Okavango Delta.

Attracted by the delta's deep waters and good fishing, Hambukushu catch fish using special baskets woven from reeds growing by the river.

The delta was first home to the San people. Today their descendants share the land with many indigenous communities including Wayeyi, Batawana, Ovaherero and Hambukushu.

To the north-west of the delta in the Tsodilo Hills there are important rock art paintings that tell the ancient human stories of this remote river basin.

Let's save the Okavango Delta
because of its precious water.

The Okavango River winds slowly across Angola, Namibia and Botswana. Millions of people rely on its fresh water. Fast-growing cities and big companies are taking more and more water from the river as it flows towards the delta. This threatens to reduce the floodwater the local communities and migrating wildlife depend on each year.

The challenge in this river basin, where water is scarce and many people are poor, is to share and protect water so both nature and people thrive.

There are lots of plans for big farming projects and to build dams to create energy, which will alter the flow of the mighty Okavango River.

Indigenous communities live along the riverbanks, many without tap water, so they need the fresh river water to survive.

Scientists are studying changes in the Okavango's floodwater to work out how to protect the wilderness from development upstream.

Let's save the Okavango Delta

because of its amazing ecosystem engineers.

The daily activities of three animals shape the landscape of the Okavango Delta. Billions of tiny insects called termites build towering homes out of the mud, which form islands in the water. Hippos keep the water flowing by pushing and paddling through tangled underwater plants. Elephants pull up trees for food, creating space for smaller plants to grow. They are ecosystem engineers.

Trees and plants grow from tall termite mounds. This creates much-needed shade for animals like leopards.

When elephants eat fruit, the seeds pop out in their poo. Elephants poo up to fifteen times a day, so they plant a lot of seeds!

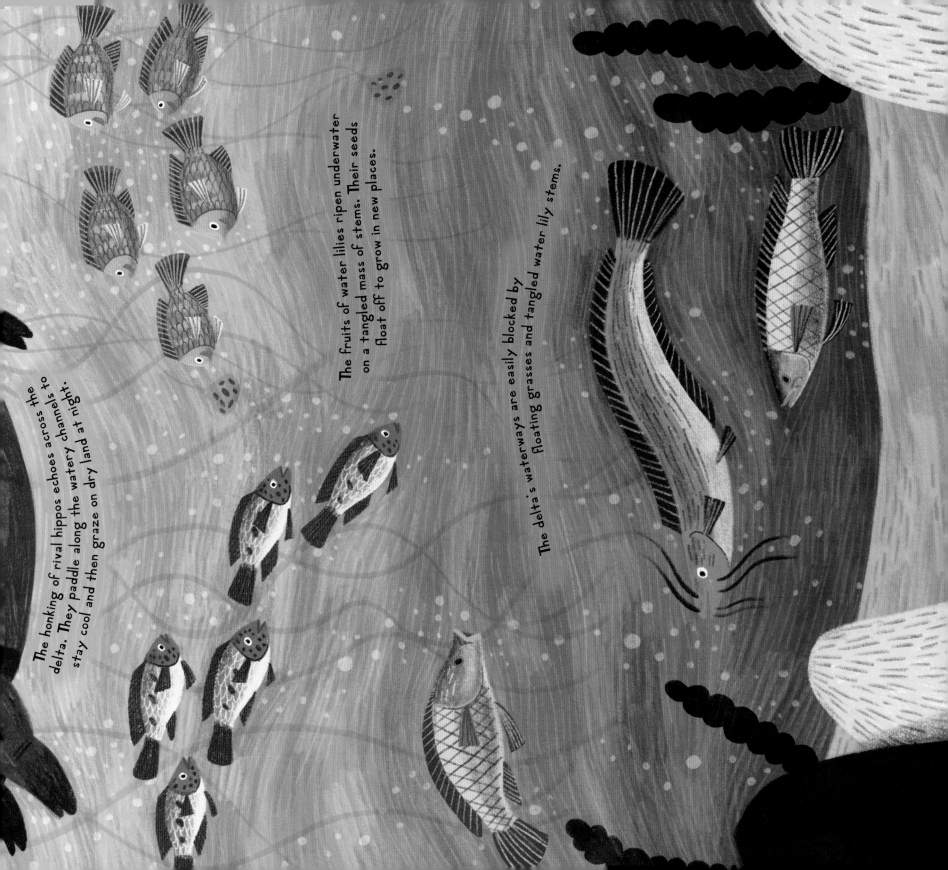

The honking of rival hippos echoes across the delta. They paddle along the watery channels to stay cool and then graze on dry land at night.

The fruits of water lilies ripen underwater on a tangled mass of stems. Their seeds float off to grow in new places.

The delta's waterways are easily blocked by floating grasses and tangled water lily stems.

Let's save the Okavango Delta
because it's a paradise

Flocks of birds, including the elegant slaty egret and wattled crane, signal the coming of the flood. They gather to feed on insects and small animals scrambling to escape the rising water. Thousands of birds also migrate to the Okavango Delta from as far away as Europe and North Africa. Plentiful food and a choice of islands to nest on mean that over 400 species of birds can be found in the delta during the flood.

At night, Pel's fishing owl dives into the water to catch fish. It can also use its large talons to snatch baby crocodiles.

The delta's famous jacana looks like it's walking on water, skipping across lily pads.

for birds.

High in the trees, the yellow-billed stork spreads its wings to shade its nest from the burning midday sun.

The Nile monitor lizard is a deadly delta predator, finding and feasting on the vulnerable eggs of wading birds.

Let's save the Okavango Delta

because it's a safari spectacle.

Visitors come from far away to marvel at the miracles of the Okavango Delta. It is one of the most popular tourist attractions in Africa. Local guides share their knowledge and bring much-needed money into their communities. Tourists arrive in planes, jump on horseback and glide on canoes to discover the delta's dazzling diversity of life.

The Moremi Game Reserve is the oldest protected area in the delta. It was the first game reserve in Africa to be established by local people.

The delta's luxury tourist camps must be very careful not to leave waste or pollute this pristine place.

During the Covid-19 pandemic, tourists stayed away, but more poachers sneaked into the swamps. Park rangers moved black rhinos to save the endangered species from the poachers' guns.

When guides tap their canoes, hippos pop up to the surface to investigate. They then steer safely between the potentially dangerous underwater giants.

Let's save the Okavango Delta

because it's an **untouched** global treasure.

The Okavango Delta is one of the biggest and most pristine wetlands on the planet. But the wilderness is threatened by big dam projects upstream and the large amounts of water taken out of the river for farming and industry. Now a new threat looms, from companies test drilling for oil. Local and global communities are demanding that the fossil fuel stays in the ground — to stop climate change and save the delta from the risk of pollution and water loss.

Oil extraction uses large amounts of water, so there is growing concern about reducing water supplies in this desert land.

Drilling for oil means more roads have to be built. This will make it easier for poachers to track down endangered species in remote areas.

Okavango communities are coming together to protect their farmland and freshwater.

LIVE THE OKAVANGO

NO OIL DRILL

LET PLANE BREATH

The migratory routes of elephants pass through areas where companies are allowed to look for oil. Underground noise caused by testing for oil may confuse these gentle giants, who communicate through the ground under their feet.

Let's save the Okavango Delta

because its swamps **store carbon**.

Like all wetlands, the Okavango Delta traps carbon. Carbon is stored in ancient plants buried deep in the peat bogs of the Panhandle, the valley funnelling water into the delta. But as global temperatures rise, the swamps will dry out and release their trapped carbon. In the air, this becomes carbon dioxide, a gas that fuels climate change.

The Okavango Delta is one of the biggest wetlands in the world so scientists know it is a very important carbon store in the fight against climate change.

Like oceans and forests, all wetlands are carbon sinks, which means they naturally store carbon, keeping it out of the air.

More than half of the world's wetlands have disappeared in the last one hundred years. These carbon-rich habitats are vanishing three times faster than forests.

Scientists are exploring the Okavango's remote swamps, mostly untouched by humans, to understand their local and global role in climate change.

permanent swamp

Panhandle

OKAVANGO DELTA

Seasonal swamp

Let's save the Okavango Delta

because it sounds the ALARM for climate change.

The Okavango Delta is in a global climate change hotspot. In the dry landscape, water is already a very precious resource. The impact of hotter temperatures will be more extreme in the delta than other parts of the world. Climate scientists believe that life in the wetlands will become more challenging. They are measuring floodwater and studying food chains to understand and protect this extraordinary place.

From tiny plankton to huge predators, scientists are studying cycles of life in the delta to understand the balance of nature.

Scientists believe climate change will alter the floods by changing and reducing the rainfall that is so critical for filling the rivers that feed the delta.

Reduced floodwater may bring fewer fish, relied on each year by local indigenous communities.

By measuring how fast water in the swamps is evaporating into the air, scientists can measure the impact of climate change.

Let's save the Okavango Delta

From a puddle to a peat bog, a ditch to a delta, or a river to a lake, there are all sorts of very different wetland habitats. In this book you have glimpsed one of the most spectacular and remote wetlands on Earth. But even at home, there is plenty you can do to protect wetlands.

Save our wetlands...

Get involved in World Wetlands Day on **2**nd February: worldwetlandsday.org

Explore your local wetlands – take a notepad to write down and draw all the species you spot.

Create your own wildlife wetland hotspot. Build a small pond at home or school and wait for creatures to arrive. Be patient – it takes time.

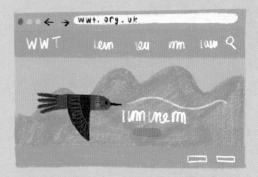

With an adult, research more about other wetlands around the world: ramsar.org   wwt.org.uk   wetlands.org

Help protect our planet...

Help combat climate change by choosing to walk or cycle rather than getting in the car, eating less meat and more vegetables and reusing, recycling and reducing the waste you create!

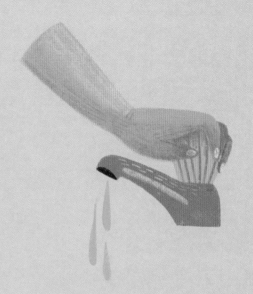

Save water at home – and encourage your friends and family too.

Stop polluting your local waterways by asking an adult if you can switch to environmentally friendly cleaning products. Never flush plasters or cotton buds down the toilet.

SAVE OUR WETLANDS

Share everything you've learned in a Wetland Wonders class or assembly.